Tea Leaves

Words by Andrew Sandner, Illustrations by Victoria Hollins

For more information or to order additional copies, please go to
www.tealeavesbook.com

This book is a work of fiction. The events and characters are a product of the author's imagination and any resemblance to actual incidents or persons, living or dead, is purely coincidental.

"Tea Leaves," by Andrew Sandner. Illustrations by Victoria Hollins. ISBN 978-1-62137-203-5.

Library of Congress Number: 2013900749.

If you have a pursuit, you must pursue it. No one is going to get it for you; you've got to get it for yourself. Instill these values in your children, and grandchildren, if or when you have them. Ensure their prosperity, and your own. Don't ever be a victim; always live fearless.

Remember... you are blessed.

CONTENTS

CONTENTS (CONT.)

Maintain Power

When rivals first meet, neither have supremacy.
View threats and vulgarity as the weapons of lesser
opponents, then smile to yourself. Such enemies are
laughable, and their words hurt like a blown kiss.
A knight won't joust a scoundrel.

BE A CHAMELEON

Adapt to the crowd and see everything. Observe the environment and secure a comfortable place. Capitalize or stay hidden depending on the ideal outcome. Blend with flowers for nectar, and muck to see slugs disappear.

DON'T SINK LOW

The most despicable are also cruel, and those who watch are equally guilty. Avoid the first and defriend the second. The bottom-feeders home is built on death and feces.

Forget Disbelievers

Some will never believe in you, and some will be
reluctant. Accept the presence of naysayers,
but listen with no ear. They themselves are afraid.
Tongues that speak through chattered teeth will
never sound quite right.

DON'T BE CLAY

Think for yourself. Act for yourself. Not every impression is for the best. When pressed by peers, don't give way. Figures molded by poor hands have cracks and brittle lives.

REJECT HATRED

Negative people are to be avoided. They soil their name and the reputations of those near. The only thing worse than being linked to hate, is to do hate yourself. Vermin spread disease, and must be shooed away.

DON'T DO STUPID THINGS

To do stupid things is to be a stupid person. Such people live lives of torment, social scorn, and self-chosen handicaps of well-deserved ends. Pain, trouble, and horrible luck teem in swamps of folly.

BE TRUSTED

Some endeavors may take some favor. The faith of others, their recommendations, and their resources are needed to see dreams succeed. Work true with those who hold power over you. The soldier proven sees promotion.

BE PATIENT

Great achievements take time, as do desirable outcomes. Don't be upset when harvest delays. It will come. Don't quit, or put out a shoddy product. Ripened fruit tastes the best.

Don't be Unfriendly

A dazed face is no better than a scowl. Greet all with kindness. Speak cordially when possible, for it brightens your aura and attracts opportunity. No one likes the droopy.

ALLOW SMALL FAULTS

Accept mistakes and small flaws in order to improve them. To be godly at everything is to be intangibly divine. No great art was never flawed.

ADAPT

Drastic changes sometimes happen. Those who cannot handle a rough transition are left behind to die. Great is the animal who survives any condition. Those who thrive in plight filled fields have time for simple pleasures.

FIGHT A CLEAN FIGHT

It is better to be beaten to a pulp, than to squeeze a flawed victory. In matters of merit, fight fierce and true. In matters of preservation, swing with a scythe.

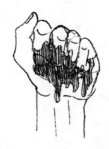

RESOURCE WISELY

Take advantage of surrounding aid. Something needed or desired may be hid nearby. Once secured, use sparingly if limited. If abundant, get your fill. The well fed fox knows its terrain.

DON'T BLABBER

"Know-it-alls" are annoying. None like to listen,
and most don't know how. Be humble and listen to
the reasoned. If knowledgeable on a topic,
wait for an opening. Aside from queries,
a head unsure keeps its mouth shut.

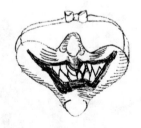

PERSIST WHEN BATTERED

Life is a gauntlet. Bruising, scaring, and broken limbs abound. The man who perseveres although hobbled, has learned much at day's end. The man who quits when thrown off course, watches others finish.

Expect Struggles

Venture out boldly, but brace for rough seas.
That way, if trouble shows its face, you can steer
around, or at least ride out the storm. Prudent sailors
pack preservers even on clearest of days.

BRING SOMETHING TO THE TABLE

Value guarantees your share and endears you to others. He who expects to eat, but didn't help prepare, relies on generosity. This may work in times of good. In times of bad, beloved dogs get fed first.

19

FAIL

Mistakes are blessings in disguise. They happen to everyone and should be embraced as friendly strangers. Don't let failure deter you. Missteps reveal dead ends and point to wiser paths. Greet defeat; then thank it for direction.

Be Self-reliant

If something needs doing, and you are able, do it yourself. This establishes you as resourceful, reliable, and invaluable. Ask for assistance only if needed. A tiger relies on itself for dinner.

MAKE YOURSELF

Focus on traits important to you. Emulate successful people with the intention to build like success. Silly people try to find themselves, like naïve seeds to fertile ground. Rootless seeds lay dormant, and even turn to dust.

HAVE SECRETS

Ideas spoken freely diminish in strength, and truths told to the daft may unravel impeccable plans. If no one needs to know, remain silent. Wounded wolves don't whimper, and deadly hunters make no sound.

AVOID LEECHES

Parasites stifle production and shrivel the flesh.
To allow such people around you ensures the loss
of assets, and the downfall of intention.
Blood runs out.

COUNT BLESSINGS

It is easy to forget how lucky you are. Be
grateful for your fortunes, for you may
have more than known. The wise,
blind man is happy to hear.

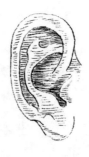

DON'T SQUANDER GOOD FORTUNE

If you are blessed enough to have Lady Luck find you, know she is easily bored. Fear only poor plans, and forget about rivals. When your song is played, dance.

HAVE A BROAD PALETTE

Try diverse things with an open mind. It is fine to have particular tastes, but don't be prissy when presented something new. The uncultured scoff at variance, and are usually a bore.

Don't Waste Time

Time is valuable property given once at birth. Some have more than others, but no mystic can say who has how much. Pursue goals as if you have little. Spent sand is spent once.

DON'T FUSS

Everyone has something to complain about. Suck it up and endure. No one expects you to whistle, but don't plague instead. It's contagious and kills the yield. Woeful stock is used for mulch.

HALT ENVY

Some will always have more than you. To guess on less favor is futile. Rather, rise toward what you want and see it through. To wonder without action, is to dream while you're asleep.

NEVER GRANDSTAND

Those who boast thirst praise from others. Such braggarts drip self-doubt. True prominence isn't promised, and is purely earned through merit.

GUIDE EXPECTATION

Certainty needs not hope, and hope is never certain.
Until it has happened, it may never happen.
Don't hope blindly in outcomes. If you feel a
need to pray, pray twice for strength.

STAY COLLECTED

It will either work to design, or it won't. A strained soul results in poor health. Few things are of dire consequence, and man is equipped to handle each. To rebuild fortune, is to become rich twice.

DECIDE SLOW, ACT FAST

Work immediately on well-conceived plans.
Do the reverse and suffer sure ruin.
Consider, choose, then checkmate.
A perfect web is a one night weave.

LET WOUNDS HEAL

There is no reason to revisit the failings of friends, or even enemies. Be silent and let the pained recover. They are more dear healthy and will be indebted for your tact. A soft touch could unclench a hardened fist.

THE SAME DIRT

No one is better than you, and you no better than they. What one man can do, you can do too. Always believe in yourself. Not all stones look the same, but all their worth need quarried pain.

Buy Granite, Afford Marble

During ascension, only purchase what is needed to build fortune. Later, once labor is paid and investment returns, secure whatever you want. Dull city walls, provide for pointed towers.

FORGET LOOKS

Appearances should be questioned. Often times they are misleading, or at worst a fake. Look twice then trust the gut. First impressions trick intention, and bait a well-set trap.

SECURE PROTECTION

Nothing is more precious than life; nothing more important than freedom. The nefarious will try to steal them away. Take measure to acquire proper defenses and remain eternally free. Fortify your castle; fill-up many quivers.

Don't Cheat

Most cheats get caught. Inevitable losses are worse
than potential gains, and sparse slumber ensues.
Cheats who sleep well are repugnant creatures.
An unearned win is a shameful lot.

ACTION OVER WORDS

Men who produce speak briefly. It is easy to talk about desires, but attainment requires executed work. Chitchat makes for nothing. Estates are built with hands of labor, not with mouths of gab.

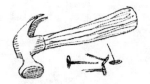

BUILD GREAT FIRE

No goal happens without the desire to see it fulfilled. One must stack true conviction. The stronger the desire, the faster flames mount. Ideas are flint for bonfires; ambition is the fuel.

TRUE PRESTIGE

There are no props for being poor, nor honor in having wealth. Rather what a man chooses to do with his time determines his worth. Affect a life for consequence; affect it well for eminence.

POLITICS

A man's politics does not encompass his soul.
Most have the best intentions for their fellow neighbor.
Many times, it's only the approach that differs.
Fair dissent is left on tables right near broken bread.

DEBT BY GREED

44

Never take if compensation owed cannot be paid.
Proper reimbursement should be prompt.
Men who eat or drink for free, owe someone
somewhere something.

ALLOW EMOTION

Moments of delight should bring smiles; moments of sadness, tears. To concern oneself with the judgment of others is to be a coward. Laugh with the loved, but cry when they're buried.

KILL DOUBT

*Have faith in your undertakings, and be confident
in their outcome. Understand good actions
benefit others. Only sacrifice is nobler.
Wage wars of the soul, then win.*

EXPLOIT SECOND CHANCES

Opportunities to correct past mistakes are seen rarely, but offered often. Seize such happenings with true vigor and leave the matter firmly in your favor. Forgiveness is given to the atoned.

DON'T BE DISLIKED INTENTIONALLY

Embrace who you are, but don't scorn the gatekeepers. They are everywhere if observant. The drawbridge locks for vagrants, but lowers for the valued.

LEARN MUCH

A man of broad knowledge is invaluable. The
more one knows, the greater his worth. To find
a foreign subject is be given a chance to learn. Regard
elders for their depth, not young men for their brawn.

SOME DIE OUT

Natural laws were written long ago. To ignore them is to spit on reason. Not every animal is long for this world. Mimic the elite, not the near extinct.

SPECIAL THANKS

GOD- THANK YOU FOR ALL I HAVE.

MELISSA JO, KACIE, MOM, AND DAD-
THANK YOU FOR THE SUPPORT, AND ALL YOUR LOVE.

VIC- THANK YOU FOR THE PATIENCE.

SEAMUS- THANK YOU FOR THE INSIGHT.

ERIK AND BOB- THANK YOU FOR THE TECHNICAL
CONTRIBUTION.

IKARUS DOWN- THANK YOU FOR THE USE OF "LOOSE SOUL."

CPSIA information can be obtained at www.ICGtesting.com
Printed in the USA
LVOW120954110313

323642LV00002B/45/P